Comments from some of Marilyn's clie

"I am moved to provide the highest recommendation for Marilyn. I have had the privilege of working with Marilyn for the past few years. She has done a wonderful job of developing my personal website. My site is highly complex — involving many articles, interviews, and videos. She has done a great job of making it user friendly.'

'I have received feedback from hundreds of people about my site. It has all been very positive! Marilyn deserves much of the credit for this success. Along with her great technical job in developing my site, Marilyn has been a pleasure to work with."

Marshall Goldsmith
Best-selling author: *What Got You Here Won't Get You There, Mojo!*
www.MarshallGoldsmithLibrary.com

"Marilyn McLeod is one of those rare people who has the ability to see potential beyond the obvious, and to bring seemingly unlikely factors together in unique solutions. She does this with a grace and respect for all involved, bringing out the best of the people around her."

Gary Ranker
The Corporate Politics Coach, Forbes Top 5 Coach
New York and Australia

"There are coaches who will stir up your emotions, give you an assignment and make you feel as if you can accomplish anything, but when the work is in front of you, and the emotion is gone, you wonder where the power you felt went and you feel you are right back where you began. Not with Marilyn McLeod.

Marilyn is an excellent business coach. She listens to you, your vision for your company and then with her expert business knowledge guides you to fruition. She asks you the important business questions you may not have considered or overlooked because of the variety of actions you must complete. Her guidance, business acumen and insightful information sets you on a path from overwhelm to achievement and growth."

Victoria Medina, Professional Actor and Photographic Artist
Numina Images, New York, New York

Also by Marilyn McLeod:

Conscious Networking
Finding and Creating Your Ideal Communities

Peer Coaching Reference
Extending Your Coaching Dollar

Recession or Plenty
7 Steps to Success in Business & in Life

Secrets of Self Publishing
Digital Tools for Publishing and Marketing

Social Media Series:

Social Media for Beginners
Step by Step for Small Business

Social Media for Small Business
Tips for Using Your Time Effectively

How to Work with Your Web Developer
Asking the Right Questions

Social Media Strategy
Navigating the New World Online

Social Media Workbook
Creating Your Master Plan

Social Media for Coaches

STRATEGIC COMMUNICATION ONLINE

by Marilyn McLeod

Social Media for Coaches
Strategic Communication Online

Library of Congress Catalog Card Number

International Standard Book Number
9781449981600

Printed in the United States of America

Social Media for Coaches
Strategic Communication Online

This book revisits the relevant points in my *Social Media for Small Business Series* and *Recession or Plenty: 7 Steps to Success in Business & in Life* through the lens of an independent business or life coach.

Quickest route to something usable in this book:
Chapter 2: Creating Your Online Plan (page 9)

It's important to be judicious in how you use these online tools, and to create a strategy that helps you accomplish your goals and doesn't waste your time. Take what you can use now and leave the rest for another day. And remember to have some fun!

The social media landscape changes very quickly, so look for updates in future editions of this book and follow me on Twitter @marilynmcleod. You'll find a link to the social media book series Facebook fan page via www.CoachMarilyn.com.

Enjoy the book and your adventures in social networking!

Join me online as we learn more together:
www.CoachMarilyn.com

Marilyn McLeod
San Diego 2010

Acknowledgements

Thank you to Anna Marie Valerio, Jeanell Innerarity, Pat Neagle, Scott Kelman and Victoria Medina for your feedback on the parent book to this series. Thank you also to Dale Biron for calling at just the right time with questions about social media … the day I'm putting together the outline for this book!

Thank you especially to my customers, my followers, subscribers and fans, who inspire me to give my best. And I hope you know … I often learn as much from you as you learn from me!!

Marilyn McLeod
February 2010

Acknowledgement

Introduction

As an independent coach you're already plenty busy. Don't expect to use everything presented in this book. If you think you have to do it all, it can be overwhelming. No one can do it all. No one needs to do it all.

If you're a beginner, let me assure you. Everyone is a beginner at some level when it comes to the Internet. Sure, I've been focused on Internet technology and online marketing since 1996, so I suppose I could call myself an expert. Does that mean I know everything about the Internet and computers? Not by a long stretch. My knowledge is broad, from how to run a web server to how to add video and optimize content for the web. Many of my colleagues focus specifically on one technical slice of the spectrum for their entire career.

Does that mean they know everything about their small niche? I watch them continuing to study while their technology of choice evolves or gives way to something new, and as the technical or social landscape around their chosen field changes.

My point is ... we're all still learning. So if you're new to this, have hope! Just take one small piece at a time, and even while you're still feeling somewhat lost and overwhelmed with the many possibilities opening up to you, you'll also be surprised at how quickly you become an expert in the eyes of people around you who know less than you did before you read this book and started playing with the ideas.

In this book I'll present a basic social media approach so you can get the lay of the land and decide where to begin. Some of the specific features I mention may have changed by the time I finish writing this sentence. If my instructions don't match your experience, look around the interface in case they moved the link, or step back and think of the general concept and see if there's another way to do what I describe.

This book can help you get started. If you need more support, check my website for webinars, teleclasses and coaching opportunities.

Marilyn McLeod
www.CoachMarilyn.com
@marilynmcleod

About the Author

Marilyn McLeod has been working with online marketing since 1996, following the changing landscape of websites, search engines, directories, news groups, online communities, blogs and social media tools. Studying a broad range of technologies along the way from the nitty-gritty of how to run a web server to how to style a web page, she's applied her knowledge to her own small business and helped other business owners to improve their online presence.

Marilyn has worked with Marshall Goldsmith since 2002 and continues to run www.MarshallGoldsmithLibrary.com. Having worked with Marshall and met his colleagues including Paul Hersey, Frances Hesselbein, Alan Mulally, Nathaniel Branden, Ken Shelton, Kevin Cashman, Robert J. Lee, John Byrne, R. Roosevelt Thomas, Jr., Ken Blanchard, Gary Ranker, Jim Goodrich, Srikumar S. Rao, Joel Barker, Chris Coffey, David G. Thomson, Sally Helgeson, Cathy Greenberg, Steve Rodgers, Frank Wagner, Denise Sinuk and many others has given her a broader social and organizational context within which to build social media applications.

She continues to refine her online and social media marketing knowledge by studying current trends and learning from her clients!

Table of Contents

CHAPTER 1

You as a Coach

ॐ

You may think your product or service is your starting point, but your key is closer to home. You are the one who will be putting in the long hours to bring your vision to fruition. You have to be healthy to carry this responsibility, and you have to be happy to carry it long enough to make it work.

What makes you happy? What do you especially enjoy doing, and who do you most like to spend time with? What are your values? What roles most appeal to you? Define a role, career, product or company that matches who you are authentically as closely as possible.

As a small business owner, you are the most valuable resource your business has. Without you, nothing in your business happens. Your health and happiness are a primary consideration in the long term success of your venture. Creating a life close to your values helps your happiness level.

We get so busy in our lives doing what we're supposed to do, carrying out tasks handed out by someone else, that it's easy to lose track of our own values in terms of our goals. The more distance between what matters to us and our daily tasks as we spend our precious time, the more likely we are to become tired and discouraged, and the more likely to lose focus, burn out and forget why we're doing our work.

Happiness comes from following through on what matters to you, so if you're checking off tasks throughout the day that you know build on what you care about, it'll go a long way toward increasing your enjoyment of your day. Your authentic level of happiness comes through as you talk with clients and prospective partners. People are attracted to sincere happiness and confidence.

First take a step back and get clear on why you're doing all of this. A clear focus will increase your ability to become someone important to the people who matter to you.

What is your primary goal?

- To increase traffic to your website or blog

- Get people to take a particular action

- Improve your visibility, credibility and authority

- Increase incoming links for SEO

- Add to what people find about you when they do a search on your name

- Boost your audience

- Attract new prospects or make sales effectively

- Interact and build a community

- Enhance your credibility and reputation

- Build your expertise and thought leadership

Who are you as an individual?

How do you want to be seen personally and professionally? What is your brand? What is your product or service? When you write in the social media arena, write from that perspective. Choose your core message, so you have a focus as you make choices and decide what to share and how to share it online. What message would help you be seen as the go-to person in your niche? Ask yourself if you're really a top player in your niche, and if you're not, what would it take to become the top player? Is the cost of gaining the fame worth what you'll accomplish as a result of your efforts?

What do you need?

I suggest you have an idea of what you want long term (this comes out of your core values), and also what you need in the immediate future. See if you can find a way to satisfy your top three needs now in such a way that it builds stepping stones toward what you want long term.

Some needs you may have as you begin your venture:

- Money
- Credibility
- Network, friends
- Something specific: place to live, service you need, people to follow your cause, etc.

What's Closest to Money, or ...
(fill in your top need, and your customer's top need)

You probably have a long list of products or services you can offer. If not, take some time to brainstorm and come up with a long list, unless you're already quite focused and know exactly what you want as an outcome of your social media efforts. Be flexible in your thinking. How can you adapt your current expertise to your customers' world?

Here are some practical questions that can help you choose which product to focus on first:

• What products/services/concepts that your target audience is ready to buy, are closest to your number one need or goal?

• Which are most fully formed and ready for market?

• Which will take the least amount of effort and resources to deliver to your customer?

• Which are easiest for your customer to understand and adopt?

Start with low-hanging fruit. Identify your top 1-5 products/services/concepts in order of which will fulfill your most important needs in the shortest amount of time with the least amount of effort.

Your Niche and Your Ideal Day

- Have you ever taken time to consider how you would spend your ideal work day if you could?

- Would you start work in the early morning or work late into the wee hours?

- Would you be surrounded by people or safely isolated behind your desk?

- Would you arrive to a full schedule of appointments or just show up and respond to the day as it happens?

- Would you have a trusted support team or be able to take care of everything yourself?

- Would you be the expert or the person supporting the expert?

- What qualities would your ideal work environment have?

- What would you accomplish each day? ... for yourself? ... for your client?

It's worth taking time to get really clear about this. You may not be able to experience your ideal day tomorrow, but you'll be surprised, as you get clear and admit to yourself what you truly value and enjoy, how circumstances can bring new opportunities and circumstances your way that begin to fit your hopes and intentions.

You and Social Media

As a small business, you're especially close to the bottom line so you're always trying to do more with less. I know you want to get more marketing exposure with fewer ad dollars. I know you also want more results with less effort because you're already too busy. The promise of social media is free advertising to reach an unlimited audience. The cost in dollars is usually free or very low. The cost comes in as time invested. I'm writing this book to help you use your limited time in the most effective way to support your business and personal goals.

This is a very social environment. As a small business it's easier for you to blend into the social media world because it's really about individual people. The culture is casual and personal. It's about being authentic, humble, relevant and helpful. Large corporations often have a social media presence, but it's about their brand. They have individuals posting for them, which is useful and often very effective, but as a small business or entrepreneur your business is probably closely associated with you as an individual, so social media is a more natural fit.

If you use your company brand and logo, be sure to put a face to the voice of the person who's speaking for your company. A good example is @ScottMonty, who is the social media voice for Ford Motor Company on Twitter.

What makes social media so effective is it's set up to be viral. It's communication and integration on steroids. If your followers, friends or connections like what you've sent them and think it'll help their network, they'll pass it along, giving you credit (at least that's the overall culture of the social media world). You provide valuable content that people want and this naturally creates awareness for whatever your business model is.

People want to be heard. If you respond to them with interest and appreciation, it shows them they've been heard, and they'll want to give back to you.

Because your social media efforts allow you to keep your name and information in front of more people each time you post a new message and possibly long after, social media can help you retain people in your network. You can energize a certain number of them to take action. You can find new people to add to your network.

Your contributions and presence can enhance your reputation as a reliable authority in your niche and help establish your brand based on your expertise.

As you present yourself and make connections and friends online, you show them how to find your online home base so they can get to know you better. You can then lead them to your offerings and give them a clear way to respond and ask for what you offer. If you hear back any comments that sound critical, open your heart, be authentically curious, and reflect on the need behind their comment.

They've just given you their consulting services for free. Look for the nugget behind the style of their message for how you might tweak what you do to become even more unique and valuable in your field (see Chapter 8: "Universal Needs Chart" page 91).

CHAPTER 2

Creating Your Online Plan

ℰᴐ

I've written this chapter to be used as a workbook. I've left space for you to jot down notes you can refer to later as you create your strategy.

First, don't be afraid to claim a niche. Avoid being too general. Make a statement from your point of view, from what you know and what you care about. Focus on your original ideas. Help people solve their problems.

My Niche:

What do you want people to do when they find you? You'll want to provide a clear call to action on every post, every website, social media site and message you put out there about you and your business.

My Call to Action:

The first step in presenting yourself online is to know how you want to be seen. This may seem simple at first glance, but it may take some time to become clear. Don't use not knowing exactly what you want your image and message to be yet as an excuse for doing nothing. We all learn as we try things online. Join the conversation and be one of the peeps helping our online world evolve!

My Online Image:

Who do you want to interact with online? Customers, prospects, thought leaders, influencers, peers, competitors, random people you may meet, existing friends? What demographics are important to you?

My Target Audience:

What key messages do you want your customers to hear? You want to be seen as providing excellent content to your readers, and not just noise.

My Key Message:

Write a paragraph or two describing your offering, or make a list of phrases you can draw upon. Use benefit statements.

What's in it for My Audience:

How I Want to Engage with Social Media:

☐   As a fly on the wall

☐   Interacting with current customers

☐   Recruiting new customers

☐   As a one-way distribution channel

☐   Power networking

☐   Provide support

☐   Brand or reputation management

Other:

Optimizing

Find your top 5 search phrases and incorporate them into your bio and key messages about you, your products and services. Add the keywords in context, so your message makes sense to your readers.

Find your search terms by doing the following:

☐ Write down the terms you think potential clients are typing into search engines to find what you offer.

☐ If you have recently gained some new clients, ask them how they found you. If they found you online, ask them if they remember what words they typed into the search engine to find you.

☐ Go to search engines like Google.com, Yahoo.com, MSN.com and Bing.com and type in these search terms. How many pages come up? Are the type of websites that appear on page one of the results closely related to what you do? Write down the search words that seem most effective, even if they have an enormous number of competitive websites in the search results.

You've just discovered something about the supply of web pages that compete with your message.

My Top 5 Search Phrases:

CHAPTER 3

Social Media Basics

ℰↄ

Social media is a set of online tools that facilitate conversation and networking with people you know, and people you have yet to meet. The tools are usually neutral, simply providing functionality. It's often how the users interpret and apply the tools that determines how they evolve over time.

What are Some Social Media Payoffs?

- Have you lost touch with people over the years, or even groups of people? With **Facebook's Friend Finder,** you might find them again, and connect with them in such a way you can stay in touch easily.

- Do you sometimes wish you could be a little bird on someone's shoulder to see what they're learning, what new developments they're excited about? With **Twitter** you can follow them and get real-time information as they send updates (or 'tweet').

- Would you like a website, but just don't have the money to pay a web developer, or are you tired of waiting weeks or months for your developer to finally make the few updates you want to your website? With a **blog** you can control your own updates and establish an online presence with free blog accounts.

- Would you like an easy way to message a group of people you work with? **Twitter, Facebook** or **LinkedIn** might be the answer.

You have your circle of influence. Do you ever wish you could send a message to second-degree contacts, meaning everyone connected to the people in your circle of influence? With **LinkedIn** you can do this.

Would you like a way to boost your brand without spending a lot of money? A well-designed social media campaign can make a big difference.

The Basic Building Blocks of a Social Media Campaign

Blogs and Websites

It's important to have one place online you call home. I call this your hub or home base. With the other social media tools I'll cover in this book, the length of your outgoing message is very brief. Your blog or website is where you can upload all of your cornerstone content, everything you want people to see about you and your products or services. It's where you actually sell your product if that's your goal. It's where you point your readers to find out more about you in each message you send online and offline.

Facebook

Facebook is more about connecting with groups of people. You can control who sees your status updates by accepting or not accepting friend requests. Some people use their Facebook profile account as a private forum for family members or close friends only, and some people open it up and friend as many people as they can. Another side of Facebook is the Fan Page, which is another option you can choose as your home base.

LinkedIn

For professionals who want to connect with other professionals in order to network, LinkedIn is the place to be. You can search within your personal connections to find out who might help you learn about a particular company, or find out who knows someone you want to meet. Most of what you can do with first-degree contacts is free. If you want more robust services there is a nominal charge.

Twitter

Whereas with LinkedIn and Facebook both parties have to agree to the connection, with Twitter each party simply decides to follow the other. Most messages on Twitter are available for public view, and anyone can search the database of messages whether they are signed into Twitter or not.

Social Media Strategy

The way you use these other social media sites effectively depends on you and your key audience, how much time you and they spend on computers and mobile devices, whether they prefer to read or watch videos, and what you want to accomplish. I'll talk more about strategy in Chapter 5: Social Media to Find and Support Clients.

Social Media Security

There are no guarantees regarding online security. Even some of the most well-developed websites have been hacked, and whenever there is a password there is at least someone who gives their password to someone else, writes it somewhere anyone can find, or someone else with a software program that can break the code and get in somehow to gain access to sensitive information.

You're always running some kind of risk when you put your information online, but by the same token, you're running nearly the same risk when you engage in any transaction in our modern society because transactions are usually carried via Internet connections, even by local merchants. Your photo may be stolen from a website and used elsewhere, but as you're walking in public someone can take your photo with their cellphone and have a better quality photo to use as they will. It's just part of our modern society.

Part of security involves who owns your content when you put it online. It's likely Facebook or Google.com or others may at one point say they own whatever you upload to their website. Read their terms of service or get legal advice if that's important to you.

One way to look at this is, rather than be worried about who's going to find out what about you online, take control of the message. Remember, anything you put online is likely to be found when someone does a search on your name or your brand. Think about this before posting. How will this look to my future employer, my children, my grandmother? Does this post carry the message I want people to know about me? If you're angry or had too much to drink, wait for the occasion to pass and write your post when you're back to yourself again.

Social Media Etiquette

It used to be when we were in meetings, if someone was bored or tuning out you couldn't always tell. Now it's very easy to tell when someone isn't paying attention when they're looking at their Blackberry, reading or texting messages, or even worse, answering their phone and having their conversation while still in the meeting. It's just rude. If you're in a meeting, be in the meeting. If you need to respond to a phone call or message, let the people in the meeting know you're expecting a call and politely ask to be excused, and then get back to the meeting as soon as you can and catch up so people know you care. You're managing others' perception of you as well as doing business in the meeting. If you're bored in the meeting, find some way to make it interesting and useful.

If you're basically a techie and spend most of your time away from people, you may be more comfortable with your Blackberry in the meeting than with the people in the meeting. Your social skills with people may be a bit rusty, and you may notice people don't know how to communicate with you. Try to improve your offline communication skills if your work brings you in contact with other people. Slow down, take a deep breath, and listen. Try to understand what they're saying and what they want. They may perceive you as someone who just pushes your technical solution which doesn't make sense to them. Listen to them with the intention of sincerely trying to understand from their point of view, and have a two-way conversation where you repeat back to them what you heard them say until they agree you understand. The points you'll gain with your colleagues can be enormous. Once they know you're both on the same page and they sense you understand them, they'll be more likely to listen to your technical solutions. You may even be able to make some important adjustments to your original technical design or procedure based on what you've learned in the conversation.

Social media etiquette in general: It's a lot like what I described in the previous two paragraphs. Online social skills are very similar to offline social skills. It's listening first and responding to their needs, making the connection and gaining rapport and trust before we broadcast our own message. It's more about conversation than about pushing what we want to say.

When you go to a social media website, look at how people are relating to each other. Each social media site has its own culture and its own rules. Become acquainted with both, and follow their lead as you introduce yourself on their site and interact with their members. When you post, write to that audience, to their needs and concerns, in the language and in concert with the values of the culture.

Keep your standards high when you post on these sites. Always be respectful. Come from a place of sincerely wanting to help other members. Think before you post. Post when you have something of value to contribute.

Remember to check in with yourself for some objectivity about your personal ups and downs before going public with a statement. If you're out of sorts and you feel compelled to send a tweet, don't. If you're angry or upset about something, wait until you've calmed down and can be clear about what you really want, then make a clear request that will help you get what you want. Tweets and posts last. Think of how you want to be seen in the future before you hit the 'send' button. Is this something memorable and of value? Is it something you'll be proud of in the future?

CHAPTER 4

Your Ideal Client

ℰↄ

You can choose your customers and you can change your customers. There are many important characteristics of good customers: They need and value what we offer, they can afford our services, and they pay their bills on time, for instance. Another way to look at this: Find customers you really enjoy being with. This will make it a pleasant experience to serve them, because you'll want to help them anyway.

Some questions you might ask yourself:

1) Think about who you enjoy spending time with. Write down any specifics that come to mind.

2) Are there particular activities you enjoy doing with these people, and others that you don't like doing with them? Think about this and take notes.

3) What kind of people do you naturally attract? Are they people you enjoy being with? If yes, what do you like about them? If no, what don't you like about the interaction? Can you think of a way to make this win-win? Take notes.

Spend some quality time with the people you most enjoy being around and listen to them on their terms. Learn what they need, and from that perspective start thinking about what valuable improvement in their lives you can provide.

Identify Your Ideal Customer

- What are their characteristics?

- Are they avid techies or completely new to the online world?

- What are their needs?

- What do they value?

- What makes them happy?

- What do they want now?

- What do your current followers or subscribers want?

- What will interest them and solve their problems?

- Where, when and how do they shop? What do they shop for?

- How do they spend discretionary money?

- What organizations do they belong to?

- What online and print publications do they subscribe to?

- Where can you find them? Make a list both online and offline.

- Is your audience more comfortable reading online, watching videos, or listening to podcasts?

- Would they prefer educational webinars, or fun animations and clever stories?

How do they see you?

- What do your stakeholders think they need from you?

- What do you have and want to offer them?

- What do they need and value in their own lives?

If you don't offer everything your core customers want, become a resource to help them find those things.

Which audience matters most to you? Put your efforts into what adds value to those people.

What Is Your Customer's Goal?

Take a moment to think about what each of your customers want. Refer to the Feelings and Needs charts (page 91) to help you guess what specific customers may want.

After you have exercised your brain for awhile, check out your assumptions. Ask your customers what they need! Have a conversation! If you've guessed wrong, they'll correct you. They may correct you with gusto, but don't necessarily misinterpret this as meaning they're unhappy. Usually they are so thrilled that someone is finally listening to them that their excitement bubbles over with a lot of energy!

If they are unhappy or even angry and you're feeling safe enough, listen to them with sincere interest and compassion. If you can hear them out without being defensive, it could be a wonderful gift for both of you. You will probably gain some unexpected and valuable insight that will help propel your success with them and other customers. A truly honest conversation may even help you become clearer on your own personal goals. You may also possibly make a new friend.

CHAPTER 5

Social Media to Find and Support Clients

ℰↃ

For more detail on social media check out my *Social Media for Small Business Series*. In this chapter I'll give an overview of Volume 1: *Social Media for Beginners*.

Where to Start

There are many social media tools and many other online services available, most of them free. As a professional coach I recommend you start with LinkedIn, assuming you already have a website or blog as your online hub.

As you create content on social media sites, always send links back to your hub. This might be your website, your blog, or your Facebook fan page. Your hub is where you'll keep your repository of content about yourself and your product, where you can take up as much space as you need. This is probably something you'll continue adding to and editing over time.

Blogs and Websites

In case you don't yet have an online hub, I recommend you start with a blog.

A website is usually a static (meaning what you see on screen doesn't change unless you ask your web developer to upload changes to your website) set of web pages that someone can click through to find the content you've asked your web developer to put online for you.

Websites are mostly about one-way conversation. There may be some interactive sections that contain forms where website visitors can click and either ask for information, or answer questions and submit the online form to you. Unless you understand HTML and FTP you usually can't alter the content of the pages, unless you use a templated system that gives you limited access. Unless you provide a contact form on your website, your visitors can't send you feedback directly from your website.

Basically, a blog is a website. Unless you already have a website that's working for you or you have a large budget, a blog is a terrific way to create an online hub for your content. You can go deeper into your content, and answer questions you pose with Twitter headlines linking to your blog posts, for instance (more about that in Volume 4 *Social Media Strategy*. I'm trying to keep things very simple and basic in this book).

A blog is a collection of your posts, or brief articles, that you add regularly (minimum once or twice a week, or better: daily). It's set up so your blog visitors can comment on your posts, and you can respond to their comments. This structure dovetails nicely with the social media culture, which is all about conversation and developing online relationships.

Getting Started

Website

Sometimes when you register a domain name, your registrar will offer you a website template to go with the domain. Templated websites are an economical way to create a website without having to pay a web developer, however they limit your ability to be creative with the layout of your site, and there are also limitations in terms of how search engines index your pages. They do often allow you to update your own content.

Blog

You can use a hosted blog solution or ask your web developer to install blog software on your own server (see more about this in Volume 3: *How to Work with Your Web Developer*). Some hosted blog software options:

> WordPress.org
> Blogger.com
> Movabletype.org
> Typepad.com

Before creating an account, have the following ready:

- Your list of key search terms

- Your blog title (consider including key search terms in your blog title).

- A description of your blog.

- An image for your top banner (optional).

- A list of color themes for your brand (optional).

Once you've created your account, most blog software programs work something like this:

- You create a new post, then copy and paste your article into the text area box provided and click Save.

- You create a list of categories and assign a category to your post.

- You add keywords to the Tags field and click Save.

- Preview your post to make sure it's what you want to say, then click [Publish].

Of course there are many nuances and advanced options, but this much information will help you get started with your blog.

Basic Strategy

You can have both a website and a blog. You can send website visitors to your blog and from your blog to your website. If you're going to have just one and you're interested in visitor interaction, I recommend starting with a blog. You can often add 'pages' to your blog, which is different from 'posts'. Blog pages act more like website pages.

Best Practices

When new visitors arrive at your blog, you'll want them to see at a glance what your blog is about so they can decide whether or not it's relevant to them. Display 3-5 posts about your key content where it's easy for them to find and read. These can be text or video posts.

Many people say they're not writers, or they don't have time to write blog posts. If you're not a writer, perhaps you know someone who can help you. You can have someone else draft posts that you review and edit, and you can also invite guest bloggers to contribute posts for your blog.

As you publish your blog posts you build credibility, expertise and thought leadership which can lead to sales, joint ventures, media exposure and other opportunities.

You can get free versions of blog software that are already connected to search engines, making your content easier to find through free organic search (as opposed to 'pay-per-click' advertising).

You can update your own content. You don't need a webmaster unless you want advanced options beyond the basics.

Your blog posts are automatically catalogued for visitors to view in the future. You can often assign categories which appear automatically in the navigation as you assign these categories to posts you publish.

Through comments you can engage in a dialog with your blog visitors, exploring the topic together, and converting some of those readers into leads, prospects, and customers.

Depending on the blog software you're using, you may be able to pre-schedule your posts. It's also a great way to save ideas and articles for future posts, when you save them as drafts behind the scenes.

You don't have to wait for a publisher to decide to publish your content … just create a blog and start publishing yourself! It's another form of self-publishing!

LinkedIn

LinkedIn is a community website used by professionals to keep track of their professional contacts, to research contacts and companies, to meet people and network with other professionals.

Getting Started

- Go to www.LinkedIn.com

- Under the heading: Join LinkedIn Today

- Use your own real first and last name when you sign up.

- Use your own personal email address (more about this later).

- Use a password you'll remember.

- Click the button: Join Now

You're then taken to your new LinkedIn account. You'll see several links across the top of the web page. Because this is a book for beginners, I'll just take you through the basics. Refer to other volumes in this series for more information about how to use the other links, or explore on your own … after you create your profile!

Profile

- Click on Profile, then Edit My Profile

- Add your current and past positions and education.

- Customize privacy other settings by clicking here:

  Edit Contact Settings
  Edit Public Profile Settings

Your profile is very important because it's where other professionals will look to learn more about you. You want to make a good first impression, and you want to use relevant search terms in your profile because that's what LinkedIn scans when someone does a search.

To be listed in the relevant searches for your field, be sure you've included relevant key words and phrases in your profile. Is your title a key phrase someone would type into a search box?

The reason I suggest using your own personal email address rather than the company or organization you're currently involved with is: If you move to another company, you may lose your LinkedIn account and all of the valuable contacts and history you've built up there if you've used your company email address.

List your company as your current position, but your LinkedIn account is about you. Make your profile about you rather than your current position.

Be sure to add a company profile for your company if you're a sole proprietor, or if your company isn't already listed.

Summary and Specialties

Be prepared with a robust bio including a story about how you've helped a client or organization, and a list of your previous positions. Make it clear who you are and what you do. Make it look 'on purpose'. Don't just copy in your resume; make it readable and engaging; include brief stories in the summary area.

Also have a list of names and email addresses handy for building your personal database of connections. Keep growing your network.

Basic Strategy

You can invite people to connect with you on LinkedIn, and you can choose whether or not to accept invitations from people who invite you to connect with them on LinkedIn. If you or they choose not to accept the invitation, neither of you will be part of each other's first degree contacts.

Important Note: Think carefully before inviting someone to connect with you through LinkedIn. If you send out the invitation and decide later to uninvite them (or 'withdraw' your invitation), it shows up on their history just that way. Every time they look at the link in their profile that shows your invitation it reminds them you chose to uninvite them. If you don't want them to have second thoughts about you or if you don't want to have to explain this later, think first before you invite someone to join you on LinkedIn.

Also Note: By default every time you edit your profile or connect with someone new, it goes out on a feed to all of your first degree connections as part of their regular 'LinkedIn Updates" email, so make these changes to your profile strategically.

First degree contacts are free. You can upgrade if you will be communicating with a lot of people outside your network. Most of what you can do in LinkedIn will have you searching and interacting with your first degree, personal connections.

Going beyond your personal connections, you may know someone who knows someone who either knows the answer to your question, or who can introduce you to someone at the company you want to explore.

What you can do in LinkedIn:

Search

Search your database, your personal connections:

[People, Advanced Search, Reference Search or People Search]
[Companies, Search Companies or browse industries by category]

Answers

Post questions or look for questions you can answer. Get your name out there regularly so people know who you are and what you do. Help people and deepen your connections. At this time you can only email the question to 200 of your first-degree contacts. If you have a large network, send out questions more often and rotate the recipient list.

Examples of questions: I'm ___ and I'm working on ___. Can you give me some examples of best and worst? ... an inspirational story? or 'Do you have any advice on ___?

Contacts

You can export your contact (or connections) list into an Excel spreadsheet or csv (comma separated values) file. You can import the csv file into many CRM (customer relations management) applications you use to keep track of your contacts, though you may need technical help the first time. Start keeping track of relevant information you discover about people as you build your relationships. If you keep this information in LinkedIn and the person disconnects with you, you've lost all of your notes unless you've backed up your data regularly by using the export function in LinkedIn.

Tip: When you're downloading your contacts information and you have the opportunity to give the file a name on your computer, add today's date to the name of the file, for instance [LinkedIn-2010-01.xls] and remember to save in your Data sub-folder so it's easy for you to find it later.

Recommendations

Give recommendations regularly. Sometimes your contacts reciprocate. Ask for recommendations from people who know you personally and professionally: peers, direct reports, customers and managers.

Best Practices

Make your profile look 'on purpose'.

In the name field, put just your real name. This will make it easier for people when they export their contacts and add them to the software they use to keep track of their contacts. Make it easy and clean for them by just putting the relevant information into the relevant fields.

Save your creativity for the summary section of your profile. A possible exception may be the title/company section. Consider putting your value proposition here, including keywords.

Upload a professional-looking headshot of yourself with a clean background.

When sending invitations to people you think may not recognize your name initially, contact them outside of LinkedIn first to get their agreement to connect with you in LinkedIn, and then send them the invitation through LinkedIn. This way you won't have alot of people telling LinkedIn they don't know you.

Also be sure to find out what email address your new connection is using for their LinkedIn account, and be sure to provide the one you're using, to make sure you're connected through the right accounts (and not creating stray LinkedIn accounts you don't need!)

Your 3-5 line email signature becomes your micro-profile with your branding and message, so respond to everyone who communicates with you.

Be sure to export your data periodically.

Facebook

The goal on Facebook is to connect, be seen and drive your friends back to your blog or fan page so they get to know you even better.

The fastest growing demographic on Facebook is 35-54 year olds, and the 55+ demographic isn't far behind.

Getting Started

Go to www.Facebook.com.

Facebook Profile and Fan Page

There are two ways you can participate in Facebook. One is to create a personal profile account, and the other is to create a fan page. You can have one without having the other.

In order to see your profile page, people have to be signed into their own Facebook account. You set the level of privacy for your profile account. Anyone can see your fan page.

You can only have one profile account, it has to be under your real name, and it has to be about you personally. At the moment you can only have 5000 friends as part of your profile. You can set the level of privacy and who can view your profile. Some people keep their profile private for close friends and family.

You can create several fan pages, and there is no limit to the number of fans who can be associated with your fan page. You can create a fan page about your business or a cause, or about yourself.

When you go to Facebook.com to create an account, the large colored button takes you to the profile account signup. The smaller type under the button takes you to the fan page signup. For information on how to create and use a Facebook fan page, see Volume 4 of this series *Social Media Strategy*.

Profile Account

Make sure your profile is complete. Be sure to use a good head shot photo of yourself. People want to look in your eyes so they can get to know you better and see if they can trust you. Remember to use the http:// prefix on any urls you add, so they become clickable links. Every word and phrase in your mini-bio is a searchable keyword.

Basic Strategy

Update your status at least once a day. It doesn't have to take long. Sprinkle in personal information about family vacations, hobbies, travel, and interests depending on your comfort level. There is much about your personal life that should not go anywhere online. Remember your core message, your brand and your focus.

Use Facebook's Friend Finder to locate people you know, and invite them to be one of your friends. Because Facebook watches carefully for spam behavior, it's suggested you invite no more than 20 people per day through Friend Finder. Instead you can send a message on Twitter and add to your website or blog "Are we friends yet on Facebook?" and add a link to your Facebook fan page or profile. There are no limits on how many incoming invitations you can accept from others in a day. Facebook friending is reciprocal – both parties have to agree to the connection.

Facebook Ads

Facebook offers social ads that work similar to Google AdWords in the sense you're buying targeted traffic. You can drill down very specifically to your target audience, so your ads only show up on the profiles or pages that your demographic is visiting. People on Facebook are in social mode rather than search mode, so use photos to catch their attention when you can. You have to make your ads compelling to your audience.

Events

Set up events and send invites to your friends and fans. Be sure the title of your event is descriptive with the most important keywords first.

Best Practices

Think about your purpose before creating your profile or adding friend connections. Will this be a private site for close friends and family only? Then only accept friend connections from those people you want to see those private photos you're planning to post. If you don't have alot of time to keep up with status updates from the many friends you want to connect with on Facebook, then perhaps a Fan Page makes more sense for you, especially if you're primarily promoting an organization, a cause or your profession. A Fan Page has built-in capability for your fans to have discussions, and makes it very easy to send a message to all of your fans. More about Fan Pages in *Social Media Strategy*, Volume 4 of this series.

Twitter

Twitter is a very simple service that helps people share information quickly. Most popular types of content include newsworthy, informative or funny bits. You sign up for an account, find people you want to follow (meaning read their 140 character micro-blog posts or 'tweets') and interact with people who choose to follow you. It's the inventive ways people find to use Twitter that makes it so valuable.

When you follow someone, their tweets begin appearing on your Twitter page when you're logged in. Your own tweets appear there as well. This is the 'twitter stream' or 'twitter feed'. The people who follow you see your tweets streaming by in their own twitter feed. Anyone can go to your Twitter page to see you follow, for instance www.Twitter.com/marilynmcleod.

You'll see tweets that are announcements about some event, article or opportunity. You'll also see one side of conversations the people you're following are having real-time with their own followers. If you want to see the other half of the conversation, follow the person on the other side of their conversation. This means you can eavesdrop on these public conversations.

Getting Started

Go to www.Twitter.com.

Sign up for a free account and complete your profile. Choose your username carefully, because that'll be your handle on Twitter. You can have more than one username by having more than one account; you just need a different email address for each Twitter account.

Your full name will show up on your public profile page. Under description you may want to add something personal as well as professional, since the Twitter culture is about people connecting with people rather than with institutions. Use a professional-looking headshot for your photo, with a light background so it stands out in a friendly way when it's displayed as a small image next to your tweets.

Make it consistent with whatever you've chosen as your background. Under the Design tab, you can either choose one of their stock backgrounds or upload your own image. If you create your own in Photoshop, note the areas of the page Twitter uses for their logo and navigation, and keep those areas blank. You actually only have at most 300 pixels along the left. Note the background doesn't scroll so keep the height within the visible size of the computer screen (which of course varies by computer, so just make sure your valuable information is closer to the top or middle of your background image).

You only get one link, which should be the website or blog you've defined as your online home base. You add this under Settings in your profile. You can add more links to your custom background image; they just won't be clickable. This is also the place to add your email address, though it won't be clickable. Look around at some other people's profile pages and develop a sense of how you want visitors to see you when they find your profile page.

Then search for people you want to follow (see the Find People link at the top of the page). Facebook has friends, LinkedIn has connections, and Twitter has followers. With Facebook and LinkedIn if you agree to the connection, it means both parties are connected to each other. Relationships on Twitter are not reciprocal; each person decides who they want to follow. It's possible to follow someone who isn't following you, or the other way around. You can have an unlimited number of followers. There is a limit to how many people you can follow without having them follow you.

Tweeting

When you log into your Twitter page, you'll see a dialog box that asks what you're doing. It's been suggested that a more useful question to answer, that your followers may find more interesting, is 'What are you thinking?'

Basic Strategy

You can choose to unfollow or block someone who is following you. You can choose to protect your tweets from public view, so that only people whom you approve can see your tweets.

Best Practices

If your friending policy is that you follow many people, then try to keep the number of people you follow 90% or fewer compared with the number of people who follow you.

Twitter is an especially good place to use url shorteners, since raw urls can be long and wouldn't leave much room within 140 characters for a message. It's also good practice to make your message 120 characters or fewer, to make room for your followers to add something if they choose to retweet your post to their followers.

Once you post, look for replies and respond to them, thereby building rapport with the person who replied, as well as the people who are reading your conversation. Include the person's Twitter handle in your reply or comment, for instance [@marilynmcleod

Thx for the mention!]. When your followers add their knowledge to your thread, thank them for their added value and respond again, continuing the conversation. Connecting, conversations, collaborating and creativity are the essence of social media. Nowhere does this happen as efficiently as on Twitter.

Promote blog posts and articles, and also promote other people's work that you think your followers will appreciate. Not only are you providing value to your followers, the people whose content you're tweeting will appreciate this and will probably want to work more closely with you.

Put yourself in your audience's shoes. What will be valuable to them? Point them to news items, resources, reports, or other links you think they'll find valuable. Intersperse these news and resources with links to your own website. What is your ratio between messages about you (that hopefully help your audience) with messages thanking others for retweeting, acknowledging others and links to sites other than yours? There should be a balance between tweets helping other people and tweets promoting yourself. You decide the ratio. What's the best ratio? Find other people like you who are successful in your field on Twitter and check out their ratio to help you decide.

Retweeting

Retweeting is a common practice on Twitter. When you see someone else's tweet go by and you think it's especially interesting, funny or informative and you think your audience will appreciate it, just send the other person's tweet to your own followers.

Why is this a good practice? Won't they mind you 'stealing' their post? On Twitter it's considered a good thing ... if you give credit to the original author and the person who sent it to you. This is why I suggest you create tweets that are only 120 characters, even though Twitter allows you 140 characters. This leaves 20 characters for someone to add to the beginning of the message [RT @ marilynmcleod] or the end of the message [via @marilynmcleod], which preserves the compelling headline you wrote.

Following

Who you choose to follow, how many people you choose to follow, whether or not you create lists of the people you follow ... that's all entirely up to you.

Here are some steps to help you manage this process:

Set your Twitter preferences to receive an email notification whenever a new person follows you. When you receive a notification go through the following steps keeping your friending policy (page 18) in mind to decide whether or not to follow the person back:

Click on the link in the email to look at the person's profile.

Read their bio.
Look at their recent tweets to see how they're using Twitter.

Follow their clickable link.

Do they have many @ replies? Are they engaging in dialog with the community or just broadcasting their own message?

Who are they following and who follows them?

Do their connections intersect with your community? Why do you think they've decided to follow you?

To become proactive, use Twellow.com to find new people to follow.

Spam

If someone follows you just long enough for your auto follow software to add them as your follower and then unfollows you as soon as you follow them, they may be a spammer (or they may object to the content of your tweets). If you see someone following you who's selling porn or is obviously spamming, follow twitter.com/spam and send @spam a direct message with the spammer's @ name.

Direct Messages

DM's (direct messages) are explained in Volume 4 Social Media Strategy because I consider them advanced ... it's easy to mistakenly send a direct message that you think will be private and have it go out to all of your followers as a public message. Perhaps by the time you read this Twitter will provide an easy way to send a DM through their website interface. In the meantime if you're using a third party application it's possible they make it easy for you to DM.

Other Social Media Options

Among the myriad social media sites and tools available online, following are some other strategies you may find useful.

Articles Marketing

People go to the Internet to get free information. When they find the information they need on your website, or in an article linking to your website, you're establishing rapport and trust, which is the basis of social media and new clients. Hopefully they'll give you a link from their website or social media post, or send an email to some friends or even clients.

You want your content on as many high traffic Internet sites and ezines as you can. If you're a writer, consider writing articles you give away to websites that specialize in providing content to webmasters and other site owners. Why would you do this? Because it helps position you as an expert in your field (when you write about content in your field), and because you get a resource or signature box at the end of the article where you can put a link back to your website along with your contact information.

When other site owners decide to use your content you get more incoming links to your own website, which helps you appear higher in search engine results, and also puts your name in front of a whole new audience that you don't even know. All for free, so everybody wins.

By the way, when someone writes to ask you if they can publish your content, thank them! Then ask for permission to add them to your list of online publishers, so you can send them an advance copy of your upcoming articles.

Writing articles is similar to writing blog posts; in fact you may want to look at which blog posts were particularly successful and rewrite some of those as articles. How-to articles are popular because they're useful.

When you're writing articles, consider:

Revisit your notes from Chapters 1 and 2 about yourself and your audience. See Volume 4 of my *Social Media for Small Business Series* for more detail on how to create your online identity and message. Keep your desired image and result in mind as you write in a style and with information consistent with how you want to be seen professionally.

Think about the key messages you want to convey to potential clients. Choose one and come up with keywords and search terms (see Volume 1 of my *Social Media for Small Business Series*) which you can use in your headline and within the article.

- Who is your audience? What do they care about? How do they think and speak? Write in their language.

- Why would this message be valuable to your reader? Write a one-sentence benefit statement to introduce the article.

- Write a compelling headline as the title. Watch the subject line in emails you receive and notice which words or phrases catch your interest. Incorporate those ideas into your headline. Keep a list for future articles.

- Make each article about only one topic. Make a promise in a compelling headline, then deliver on that promise in your article.

- Describe the problem you're going to solve in your article. Describe what happens if people don't use the information in your article.

- Give clear solutions that lead to what you offer. Show the reader how to do things for themselves that lead to what you offer, should they choose to get more information or assistance.

- Tell a story. Did you take a client through these how-to steps? Did you learn this process through your own experience? Put a face on the message so it comes alive and makes more sense to the reader.

- End with a clear call to action. Suggest a next step, or where to get more information.

As you're writing, get to the point. When you're finished writing, print a copy and read it as though you are your target audience. Mark it up with edits to add clarity, simplify, and make sure you're addressing all of the key points. Are you speaking to their needs or rambling on some unrelated topic? Stay focused on your message, and the needs of your audience.

You don't want to just dump out what you know; you want to engage people and speak to their dilemmas. Don't lecture. Be a helpful friend or coach.

Your article should be 300-800 words, depending on the purpose. Each article must be able to stand on its own, and not depend on content from previous articles. Use Word Count in Microsoft Word to track length as you write.

Don't submit the same article to more than one portal. Rewrite your article several different ways, one for each portal.

Some reasons articles get rejected: duplicate content (use dupe-cop.com to make sure your new article is at least 50% unique compared with your previous article about a similar topic), or the article may be too short or not up to par (make sure your articles have quality content).

Submit to your article portal sites individually. Don't use article submission services. Remove outdated articles and update them. You can use hubpages.com or ezinearticles.com as a blog. As you respond to comments, you can build a community.

Tips for writing your resource or signature box: choose each word carefully and include keywords. You get only about 450 characters max. You can usually include two links in your resource box. One can be a link to an offer, the other can be optimized for search engines. Tell the reader what to do, and why. Be specific. Tailor the resource box to the article. Remember to answer your reader's most basic question in whatever you write: "What's in it for me?"

Bookmarking Sites

Social bookmarking allows people to find, record, share and discuss bookmarks. Instead of having these bookmarks reside on their home computer, they are easily accessible from anywhere because they're online and accessible from a web browser. They are also shared with anyone who cares to look.

Social bookmarking sites can be a great way to expand your reach and bring incoming links. People use bookmarking sites to speed up their research. Bookmarks are submitted by members, and members vote to move bookmarks up and down in popularity.

If the first vote is cast by a powerful influencer within the community, it carries much more weight, and because of that member's popularity, many others will be voting on your bookmark.

If you're looking for votes, the power influencers of the site are your customers, so think about what's in it for them when you ask a favor. Do a favor for them first, which might look this way: You see their link in Twitter, you like it, and you submit it to Stumble-Upon.

There are five top social bookmarking sites: Digg.com, Del.icio.us, Reddit.com, StumbleUpon.com, and Mixx.com. Each has its own culture, and before you jump in and push your own links, get to know the culture of each community, learn to speak their language, and give them what they care about.

If you submit an article that runs counter to the culture, or if one member decides to label it as porn because they didn't like it, you may experience a barrage of negative remarks and your article may go to the bottom of the list. If this happens, let it roll off your back and just move on.

It's important to be authentic to differentiate yourself from the spammers just trying to get traffic. The more real and approachable you seem, the more likely you'll build trust within the community. Avoid trying to game the system. Get to know people and gain followers.

Submit quality content. Don't just share your own. Don't just show up when you have something you want to push. Join in the discussion. Get to know people. Vote on content you find on the site. Contribute to the discussion. Be part of the community.

What does it take to become a power influencer? It happens over time as you consistently submit stories that become popular, vote early on stories that go hot, write comments that get voted up, have a lot of followers, and have a good profile consistent across various sites.

Ways to promote your own material:

Add voting buttons to stories on your blog or website (look for plugins in your blog or content management software). Give people a Twitter button to help them retweet your content.

If you ask your friends to vote, don't send them the direct url. Instead, tell them which category to click on, and then which article to click on, so they go through the natural channels of the site. Going directly to the article deep in the bookmarking site sets off spam flags.

When you submit a link and description, consider the keywords you'll use for the tags. People search for keywords and tags to find content.

Be sure to choose the correct category.

Submitting good material:

Don't plagiarize, offend, use hype, over-monetize, or spam. Obvious selling doesn't work in social bookmarking.

Turn off your pop-ups, at least while traffic spikes.

Use simple, easy to understand words.

Make sure your headlines are compelling, and they focus on this bookmarking site audience's interests and point of view.

Submit content people will want to share with their friends, or that requires a second look, or something you want to keep as reference. Look for how-to articles, lists, best/worst/most, content with a hook, something that makes you smile.

If you're writing your own articles to submit, review "Articles Marketing" for tips on writing compelling articles.

Community Sites

There are many ways to participate in existing community sites, or to create your own. Many of the larger sites (Facebook.com, LinkedIn) allow you to create your own groups within their community.

A Facebook fan page allows you to install a variety of applications to interact with your fans.

Forums or threaded discussion boards are less about long blog posts, and more about conversation. They allow longer posts than Twitter. You can change settings regarding who can read and post. Forum software is available free, such phpBB. It simply requires installation on your server.

There are also community sites like Ning.com which allows you to create your own social network. It's free if you allow their ads, and if you allow your members to create their own groups within your group. You can customize your account by paying for various configurations.

Wiki is another application which is available as a free download, and is fairly easy to install by someone who understands servers. It's often used by a community of people like a group of students taking a course, to share documents and encourage discussion among members. It can also be used like Wikipedia to display information about a topic.

Important note: If you install any of this software on your website, be sure to work with someone experienced in website security, and stay current with software updates for the application.

Email Marketing

Your first step toward online marketing should be your email signature. Include your value proposition and important website links and contact information. It's your mini-profile. Copy it at the end of messages within social networks.

With the exception of a few friends I can now reach only on Twitter, most people I know still rely on their email accounts to communicate with their co-workers and friends.

This provides an important channel for your newsletter or ezine. If you're going to send out a newsletter, provide an opt-in box for them to sign up, and give them a way in each email to unsubscribe. You can use online services to manage your subscribers and newsletter editions, or you can do it all manually using your text editor to keep track of email addresses, and paste them several at a time into the BCC: area of your email message.

To help you not look like a spammer, look through your spam filter and avoid using that style in your headlines. If you're sending manually from your own account, don't send it to hundreds of names in the same email. Do you have different groups of friends? Keep them listed this way, and send your newsletter multiple times. Some email services such as aweber.com offer autoresponders and rss to email, which can help you manage not only newsletters, but blog posts and online courses you may wish to offer.

Content is important. You'll lose subscribers if they think you're all about selling something, or if your content isn't useful or compelling. Read Articles Marketing (page 48) for tips on writing articles.

Think about your audience and what they'd respond well to: tips, articles, resources, special offers. You want your subscribers to see so much value in your ezine that they forward it to their friends. If you want to send out a newsletter and you're not a writer, consider asking associates to contribute articles. As you meet others online, you can ask permission to reprint their ideas or articles, as long as you give credit and a link back to their website.

How often to send an ezine? I suggest monthly, unless your topic requires more updates. You don't want people to get overwhelmed with another email from you they don't have time to read (so they begin to automatically trash it or unsubscribe), and you don't want to spend all of your time writing newsletters.

People are busy, so give them headlines at the top of your newsletter so they can decide what to read. You can link back to the story on your website (this is great for traffic), or you can include the article within the email (which may encourage readers to forward it to their friends, if the content is compelling). In any case, always link to your website from your ezine, and include your contact information in your signature box at the end.

Make it easy to read online, with short paragraphs and bulleted lists. Avoid quotation marks or other symbols in the subject line that might confuse or attract email spam filters. Just send simple text.

Look through newsletters and ezines you subscribe to, and notice what you think works best. Blend those elements together and create your own format. Subscribe to other ezines in your field.
In addition to sending ezines to your subscribers, you can also upload them to your website (adding valuable content), and rewrite as articles (see Articles Marketing page 48).

Teleconferences and Webinars

Increasingly companies are curbing their travel budgets. To continue educational and marketing objectives, teleconferences and webinars are becoming more popular.

Webinar software often allows participants who are logged in to view a PowerPoint slide presentation and hear the speaker's presentation. The webinar can be recorded for future use.

Polls can be used before, during and after a webinar to increase the likelihood the content will meet the audience's needs. Q&A and chat features can enable two-way communication in an otherwise limited environment.

During the conference it's very helpful to have at least one person paying attention to keeping the technology working, and monitoring Q&A and chat while the other person (or persons) are presenting. It's also useful to schedule a practice webinar with your speakers and technical people before the actual webinar goes live.

Leave the webinar with a clear message to participants about their next step. Send a follow up email the next day to ask if there were any unanswered questions, and follow up. An easy way to add value is to provide participants access to the webinar recording, at least for a limited time.

URL Shorteners

Sometimes you want a very short url because you're posting it in Twitter and you want to save characters. You may want to hide a code which is part of a url. Sometimes you just want to make the link you're embedding into an email or elsewhere easier to read. There are several websites that provide this service. Do an online search for 'url shortener'. Just paste the long url into the appropriate place, and copy the shorter url they created for you into the post you're sending out to your followers.

Video

It's much easier to display video online now than it used to be. Every time I've worked with raw video in the past, the process has taken longer than I expected because of so many variables. Now with easy video cams and websites like YouTube, anyone can do it. Choose the website you'll use and note their limitations. If the site allows no more than 10 minute videos, keep it under ten minutes before you upload. There are different formats: .avi. .mov, .mpeg etc. Export from your camera or video editing program into a format your chosen video service can accept.

Another limitation is file size. Find the file on your computer and right click on Properties (Windows) or Get Info (Mac) to find the file size. If it needs to be smaller, export it again using compression settings so it's small enough to upload. I usually keep an archive version in the large file size in case I want to use the footage in another way in the future.

There are various video players and ways to display video on a web page. One easy way with YouTube is to copy the embed link from the video page on YouTube, and paste it into the html code where you want the video to appear on your web page. It sounds tricky, but it's really pretty easy. It needs to be between the <body> and </body> tags. Or you can just link to the page on YouTube from your website, from a Twitter or Facebook post, or your blog.

You can also create your own YouTube channel. It's just like a TV channel that allows people to follow you.

Video blogs appeal to a different audience than text blogs. In fact, readers are in the minority. Know what your audience responds to. It's possible to embed a video into a text blog so you can appeal to both. Video is a great way to differentiate yourself from your competitors.

Note: If you allow video comments on your YouTube account, keep a watchful eye for voluptuous women who appear that may not convey the kind of image you want associated with your account.

Alternatives to video that also provide visual stimulation: photos, audio, PowerPoint slides, pdf files, charts, animations.

Revisit Your Goals

Before investing time and resources into a new venture, revisit your research from Chapter 1 regarding who you are, what makes you happy, your goals, and how you want your work to support your goals. Also revisit your target audience, what they want, and where to find them.

If you have the resources to repurpose your content into a format your target audience will appreciate, that supports you and your goals … go for it!

CHAPTER 6

Automating and Delegating

ॐ

This can all be very time consuming. Many of these tasks (like tweets) are very personal to you. Other tasks can be delegated to some trusted person who understands your style, your point of view and your business. Still other tasks can be automated as social media tools increasingly allow you to connect your various accounts together.

As I write this chapter I'm trying to keep it very, very basic. I also see that even the basics make a somewhat long and involved chapter. Please remember to just take what you like and can use for now, and leave the rest. Even if you only implement one part of one step, you'll gain some benefit as long as you approach this effort aligned with the image you want to convey online, and you keep in mind your overall focus for your business and your life.

What You Need to Keep

Social media is about people connecting with people, not people broadcasting their message for a one-way conversation, or for organizations disseminating their sanitized message to the masses. This means if you're going to have a social media presence it needs to be about a person. If you are the main brand of your small business, then the face and voice needs to be yours personally.

Companies whose brand is not a specific person have found success in designating one spokesperson. For instance, Scott Monty is the voice of Ford Motor Company on Ford's Twitter account. This way Ford has a consistent voice on Twitter, and people who want to connect with Ford or communicate with Ford know they're actually connecting with a real person.

If you are your company's brand but you don't have time to keep up the account personally, you may ask someone who is very familiar with you and your business, who understands your voice, to help you. In this case it's a good idea to be clear with your followers there are two of you tweeting, for instance. I've worked with Marshall Goldsmith for several years with his online presence, and he's asked me to work with his social media accounts. We make an effort to be very clear to anyone following him who is speaking when se wend a tweet. Transparency and authenticity are very important to build credibility and connection with your audience.

Beyond your face and your voice, when you think about actually sitting with your computer or mobile device to send updates and keep up with your accounts, and you consider what specific tasks to keep and to delegate, instead of thinking of this whole thing as one more project to add to your already overflowing schedule, think first about the overall function of your job and how the areas of people contact (with customers, vendors, the public in general) and market research fit into your role.

Twitter is the most dynamic, real-time free market research tool available. You can ask your assistant to provide you with daily reports of trends, and maybe that's enough. Or maybe you'll get more value from watching the actual conversations as they happen.

I'm not trying to sell you on opening up your schedule to another big time commitment. I'm just asking you to look at what you're doing now, and think about how social media might be able to streamline the way you're doing things already and put you in a position of being on top of your stakeholders' current thoughts and activities. Trying a new way of managing old tasks could prove very interesting and useful.

Blog

How often do you find yourself giving the very same update to a new person? If the update is something you'd like to be known publicly, why not write a blog post for all the world to see? You can verbally tell people about the topic, and then direct them to this blog post or page for specifics.

Do you want your stakeholders, customers, staff to keep in mind your organization's point of view, mission statement, or refer to a list of contacts or resources? Putting them where everyone can easily reference them could be useful ... if it's also a message you want out in the public. If not, you may consider adding a blog function to your company intranet.

LinkedIn

Would you find it useful to send a message to your entire professional network all at once? Would you like to stay on top of what your colleagues are up to?

LinkedIn doesn't have to take a lot of your time, and if you're a professional that depends on your professional network, it can be a great time-saver and expand your reach exponentially.

It's also a great way to keep current with address and employment changes ... to let others know about changes in your life, and to maintain up-to-date information about your colleagues.

Facebook

If your Facebook profile is used primarily for close family and friends, you can create privacy settings and only friend the people you want to see your most intimate information. With the right privacy settings it can be a great way to share photos, information and updates with people close to you.

If you prefer a more open approach, you can use Facebook to find old friends and contacts through the search engine on Facebook, and through Facebook's Friend Finder.

Twitter

Track real-time updates about your market and on the news by either going to search.twitter.com and searching on your key search terms (your company name, keywords for your industry, your name, etc.), or setting up these searches in a third-party application (go to Google, Bing or Yahoo and search for 'twitter keyword alert' to find available applications).

Help From the Internet

There are more online services available than I've been able to count. I keep a list of new sites and services I find that look useful, and the list just keeps growing. I'll present a few specifics in this chapter, with more in Volume 4 of this series *Social Media Strategy*. If you need something slightly different than I suggest, just go to one of the major search engines like Google, Yahoo or Bing and do a search for what you want. You can also sometimes find comparisons by typing in more than one name of the services into one search. For instance, if you type 'WordPress Drupal Joomla' you'll probably find a comparison chart of those three software programs. I say 'probably' because by the time you read this things might have changed.

When you come across something you don't understand, search engines are your friend. What do my web developer friends do when they come across an error message while they're developing software, or my computer hardware friends when they're troubleshooting a computer issue? They copy the error message they see on the screen, and they paste it verbatim into a search engine, and voila! Up comes a list of other people's comments who have had the exact same issue.

Use this concept as you find yourself in unfamiliar territory. Adding the word 'tutorial' to a technical word is another trick I use to find people who have generously shared their knowledge about a particular technical task. Well, sometimes they've done this so they can post their ads which they hope you'll click on so they make some money. You can usually weave your way around the ads to find the content and learn what you needed to understand. To find the definition of a new technical term, just type in 'definition' and the new word.

Blog

Publishing a blog post means it's going out to the world and potentially could be listed by search engines. This can be even more effective than a traditional press release.

There is often a section on blog software for a 'blogroll', or a list of other people's blogs that you find relevant and want to share with your blog visitors. Add blogs there you want to follow yourself (making it easier for you to find them) or add blogs strategically that will help you with your customers or stakeholders (also saving you the time of hunting for this in front of your customer).

Use keywords in your blog posts that are related to what you do, what you want to be known for, and what search terms your key potential customers are currently using. You can learn more about this in Volume 1 *Social Media for Beginners* and for more advanced information, Volume 4 *Social Media Strategy*. For now just choose some terms you think are important and add them within context to the text of your posts.

LinkedIn

If you're looking for a new expert or someone to introduce you to the right person in a new company, check your connections in LinkedIn, and look into their connections.

Expand your reach in terms of being seen as an expert by interacting in the Answers area.

Facebook

You can use Facebook as a research tool in two ways:

Sign into your Facebook account and use the search box there to find people, pages and groups within Facebook that match what you're looking for, or that may lead you to what you're looking for.

Go to Google, Bing or Yahoo and type in your search term with the word 'Facebook' at the end to find references available to the general public (people who are not members of Facebook).

Twitter

You'll be surprised at what you can learn and who you can meet quickly and personally by interacting on Twitter.

Go to search.twitter.com to find real-time and very recent posts by searching on your key search terms, your company name, your name, your Twitter handle @marilynmcleod.

Help From Your Focus

I can't say enough about the importance of knowing exactly what you want. This saves everyone so much time, especially you. There are times it's best not to have an unshakable linear focus, so we can learn and adjust our course as we go forward and the environment changes. There are also times to point the way and just plain get to the destination. If you choose a less rigid approach, just be sure to know exactly what you want, so you can refer back to where you started and your original purpose when things get confusing.

It's great to make course corrections. It's not so useful to just drift about ... unless that's your style and it's working very well for you. If this is your style you'll probably need some more grounded, linear people around you to make any forward progress ... if indeed you want to make some forward progress. Life isn't always about accomplishment. Sometimes it's just about exploring, learning, and enjoying.

Blog

Create an editorial calendar with topics that support your activities throughout the year.

Create an About page that you can show people when you're introducing them to your company. This will save you time explaining details, and give people a reference point for follow up later.

LinkedIn

Make strategic updates to let your network know of your activities and accomplishments.

Ask and answer questions strategically in the Answers section. This may help you find new opportunities or strengthen relationships with people in your network.

Facebook

To convey your focus and point of view online, as a business I recommend a Facebook Fan Page rather than a profile, which I describe in Volume 4 *Social Media Strategy*.

Twitter

Create a custom background that clearly conveys your desired image and message.

Make sure your web link goes directly to the most informative web page you have that describes your desired image and message.

Tweet from your point of view with a message style that's consistent with the rest of your online marketing. Twitter is more personal but as a business you want to remember to maintain a respectful, professional tone. Maybe a good analogy is 'business casual'!

Help From Your Systems

Do you have systems you use in your work now? Do you always have staff meetings on Monday mornings and always call your spouse at lunch to check in? Do you meet with your assistant at the end of the day to catch up on loose ends, or meet the gang after work before going home?

What's working for you now? What's getting in the way of your focus? What are you missing? Where could you use more support, more information, more resources?

Take a step back and see if you can make adjustments to your existing systems to increase efficiency, effectiveness, and enjoyment of your day.

From that point of view, is there something you're already doing that could be automated? What could be delegated to either free up your personal time or your staff's personal time? Is someone else better qualified to handle any of these tasks? What would you like to get off your plate? Could that be automated or delegated?

Blog

Create a page for each type of information you and your staff find yourselves providing to people over and over again. Answer these frequently asked questions online in one place where everyone can find them.

When you and your staff hear questions from your customers and stakeholders that you think important to clarify or highlight, write a blog post about it.

LinkedIn

Continually expand your personal network by sending LinkedIn invitations to people who have agreed to connect with you on LinkedIn (be sure to use the address you're using on LinkedIn or you'll end up with stray LinkedIn accounts), and accept invitations from people you want in your personal network.

Monitor the LinkedIn email updates and note changes to contact information for your key connections.

Download your LinkedIn contacts regularly to an Excel or .csv file. If someone disconnects from you all of their information is deleted, so a backup is important.

Facebook

Facebook profile functionality is limited, so I recommend a Facebook Fan Page if you're wanting more functionality to help you with your office systems. See Volume 4 *Social Media Strategy* for more information.

Twitter

Use Twitter to gain insight into your part of the marketplace.

When you look at the list of people who have chosen to follow you, what do you think their purpose is in choosing to follow you? What do you think they want? Is this something you want to provide? Is this an indication of a new direction you or your company may want to go?

Create 120 character posts of information you want to convey to people who may be listening. Intersperse your self-serving messages between messages highlighting other people and their ideas.

Help from Online Automation

The first step in automation is to add your photo (a professional head shot) to gravatar.com. Many sites pull your photo from gravatar.com, so if you use a consistent email address as you move around the web, commenting on blogs and joining sites, you can have a consistent image and save a lot of time by registering with gravatar.com.

OpenID is another time-saver, as well as security measure. Some sites allow you to register using your OpenID account instead of using your private password and information each time you register for a new site.

PayPal offers a similar service in terms of giving out credit card and financial information. It's an inexpensive way to receive credit card payments and build a shopping cart just by using their html code which you can develop yourself on their website. You'll just need to know where to insert the html into your web page. Your web developer can help with that, or even perhaps your web designer.

The first strategic move I recommend: create alerts on your search terms to receive an email when your search term is mentioned online. Some key services available: Twilert, Tweetbeep and Google alerts.

Another helpful service is url shorteners. Using this service gives you two benefits:

The obvious benefit is a shorter url. This is especially helpful in emails and Twitter, and especially when you have a very long url.

If the url shortener site also provides tracking, you can actually watch how many people are clicking on your link just as you would with Google Analytics.

Blog

You can extend your blog's reach by sending your blog's RSS feed through other online services. RSS is a technical terms that you don't need to understand in order to use it. Just find the RSS feed link for your blog (you can probably find this in the settings panel of your blog software), and copy it into a text file you save in your RESOURCES folder (discussed in Volume 1 *Social Media for Beginners*) for handy reference later. It's just a special url that takes people to the raw file of all your blog posts instead of the pretty interface you see when you go to your main blog site.

Create a Feedburner account and add your blog (you'll need to know your RSS feed url for this). Then find the Feedburner link and paste that into the 'subscribe to this blog' feature in your blog software. That'll send people to Feedburner's free subscription service, and you'll be able to keep track of statistics (not names of people) about who's receiving your blog feed.

There are also services like PostLater which allow you to prepare blog posts in advance and preschedule them for publication later. This can be a good strategy for content posts about topics that aren't likely to change or be politically insensitive depending on current events. Use this as an adjunct to posts you write as you respond to current events and make your own special announcements.

LinkedIn

Copy your blog's RSS feed url to the blog application in LinkedIn so your blog posts display automatically in your LinkedIn profile.

Facebook

Copy your blog's RSS feed url to the Notes tab (click on the Notes tab and look on the right side of the page for the 'edit' link) so your blog posts display automatically in your Facebook profile.

Twitter

Feedburner allows you to send your blog feed directly into your Twitter account by adding your Twitter login to your Feedburner account. This allows your blog posts to display automatically in your Twitter stream.

You can preschedule tweets with applications like TweetLater, Hootsuite and SocialOomph. As with blog posts, this can be a good strategy for content posts about topics that aren't likely to change or be politically insensitive depending on current events. You can use this as an adjunct to tweets you send to respond to current events and announcements you want to make.

Review

A diagram of the ecosystem I've described above may be helpful. Please note all of these functions are optional. To preschedule:

Blog posts: PostLater => Blog => Feedburner => Twitter

Twitter posts: TweetLater => Twitter

To post real-time simply go to the individual website and login, then send a status update:

Blog
LinkedIn
Facebook
Twitter

To Extend your Blog's Reach:

Copy your blog's RSS feed url to:

LinkedIn (blog section of your profile)
Facebook (notes tab in your profile)
Twitter (from your Feedburner account)

You can see from the above that your message can travel online very quickly, especially when you take into consideration all of the people subscribing to Google alerts and Twitter alerts using the keywords you're highlighting in your posts. This can be very helpful or very unhelpful, depending on the content and timing of your post.

If you've prescheduled a post that highlights you as a rich millionaire because of your association with a pre-eminent company and you suddenly get a Google alert that tells you the company is under investigation for tax evasion, go into your prescheduling service and don't send that post just yet. Or rewrite it to make your point in a different way.

This week when I was in my LinkedIn account I noticed a status update from a young man touting a new drinking game with a link to a video on some site I didn't recognize. I wondered how potential employers would view that post, and I wondered if he wrote that post in a personal niche networking account somewhere and then forgot he'd added the feed to his LinkedIn account.

I'll remind you again ... be careful what you post. Be sure you know the image and message you want to convey online, and try to stay on message. I'm not saying don't interact in a personal way, and I'm definitely not suggesting you stick to your sanitized message. That's not what social media and social networking is about. I am saying think before you post ... would your spouse, mother, children, or potential employer or client trust you more or less for what you're about to say? If you have even a whisper of a doubt about your intended message, make a note to yourself about what you want to say, and write the post later when you're fully conscious and aware again.

Help From Your Peers

There are ways you and your colleagues can help each other online. I'll describe this from your point of view; remember you can do the same for your colleagues.

Blog

Think of the image you want to convey online, and how your blog will help support that message. Think of people you know whose contribution you value that would also support your message, and are people who will not compete with what you're selling to your target audience. Ask them to become guest bloggers on your blog, or to contribute an article here and there. Offer to give them a link back to their website within their blog post.

Ask them to add a link to your blog on their website or to the blogroll on their blog.

LinkedIn

Watch for opportunities as you read status updates from your colleagues.

Ask for their help when you need information or resources they may have access to or own.

Create a poll to help you make a decision or take the next step in designing your new program or product.

Facebook

If you're using your Facebook profile account in a public way (which is still available only to people with Facebook accounts who are logged in), you can send a status update or message your friends via email and ask for something or provide helpful information.

Twitter

Think of who you'd like to have following you to receive your updates, and cultivate those relationships. Find their Twitter account and follow them. Give them credit within Twitter by retweeting their interesting messages to your followers, including their Twitter handle (@marilynmcleod for instance) in your retweeted message. Thank them publicly as appropriate.

I've heard of people tweeting to ask for help when they're traveling and receiving some valuable local assistance.

Also of people traveling who suddenly have time on their hands and are able to meet one of their local followers in person for coffee.

If you see breaking news your followers would appreciate, announce it through a tweet.

Follow important people in your industry and read their tweets. Respond to them, retweet with attribution, and interact with them to build trust and rapport.

Help From Support Staff

One key task someone can help you with is to monitor your online reputation and do real-time research of activity that matters to you. They can also look for new people for you to connect with, or find contact information for people you've met or been associated with in the past that you'd like to add to your current network. You can ask your staff to provide you with regular reports of what they find.

- Monitor alerts on keywords related to you and your business (Google alerts and Twilert)

- Track mentions of your company, brand, products, services, competitors, etc.

- Real-time research on search.twitter.com.

- Search directories like Twellow to find people in your ideal audience.

- Send and monitor polls.

One scenario might look this way:

- You ask Person A to track and monitor your brand and mentions of your company and your product, positive and negative.

- Person A forwards the messages they find to Person B in your company who knows that part of your company inside and out. Person B responds immediately to the tweet, or makes a comment on the blog post.

- Person B monitors online response to their comments or tweet, and looks for indications of the market changing, or new opportunities in the marketplace.

Think of any negative messages more than as just complaints to deal with. Consider them an early warning system for your organization, look for trends, and consider how your organization can adapt to address your customers' concerns and perceptions.

By the same token, it's just as important to respond to people who say positive things about your brand as it is to respond to those who complain or point out errors.

A related point which I've learned from online application developers: Instead of building out your entire widget with all the bells and whistles you're sure your ideal customers need and want, get something started and then ask them what they want. Listen to them as they use and interact with your widget. Add the bells and whistles they actually need. Interact with them and give them a voice in how your widget develops. The end product will probably surprise you, and it'll cost fewer resources to develop.

Blog

If you're not a writer you can ask someone else to draft posts for you. In order to maintain your voice, it's best for you to do the final editing before they're posted.

If you enjoy writing but can't spell and get the grammar all mixed up, you might want to do the writing yourself and have someone else proof and post for you. Unless you trust them completely, you may want to review the final before it's posted publicly.

LinkedIn

Someone else can download your contacts as a backup.

They can also monitor the LinkedIn updates email that comes through, and update any contact information changes in the software you use to keep track of your contacts.

Someone else can add your blog RSS feed to your LinkedIn profile.

Facebook

Someone else can do searches for Facebook accounts, groups and fan pages about a topic of interest to you.

They can also schedule events, place ads, and add your blog RSS feed in the Notes tab.

Twitter

You can hand someone a list of search terms and ask them to summarize what they find on search.twitter.com.

You can ask someone to set up alerts for you on Twilert or Tweetbeep.

Things to Consider

- Instead of viewing your social media efforts as one more big time commitment, look instead for ways social media can streamline tasks already taking up time in your schedule.

- What can you delegate? Can you have someone ghostwrite for you in your voice? You can have someone on your team tracking and monitoring your brand and online conversations, and moderating your fan page or group.

- You think Twitter takes a lot of time and you want someone else to tweet for you. Do you really know someone you can trust to respond as you would, with your words, with your point of view, to support your goals and your message? Do they really know you and your company that well? And will you know what "you" just tweeted if you're at a meeting and someone in the audience sees a tweet coming through from you on their PDA and makes a comment to you about it on the spot? If you have someone else tweeting for you, give them a face and have them put their initials on their tweets.

- Just remember what you're after is rapport and trust from your audience. Lack of authenticity does come through, so it's better to have fewer tweets and have them authentic, than to have lots of tweets that lower trust with your audience. You are the one with the personal touch and it's your voice.

CHAPTER 7

Time Management Tips

ℰ∂

Do you find yourself getting lost in your online experience, perhaps finally 'coming to' about 3am and then dragging yourself through the following day?

Do you find yourself avoiding the whole computer or social media thing because you just don't have time?

How successful do you feel in general in terms of using your time effectively? Do you depend on a system to keep you on track throughout the day, or do you just go out there and wing it?

Personally I find I'm more effective when I have clarity. The more unknowns, especially about which next steps I expect of myself, the less I'm able to focus my resources effectively and the more I find myself staring into space or engaged in what may seem like useless activities. Sometimes a 'useless' activity actually gets me off the treadmill long enough to mentally process experiences of the day and is highly valuable, and sometimes it just uses up my valuable time.

Clear Your Mind

Make a list of everything on your to-do list. Include everything you can think of you're responsible to carry out. If it's overwhelming to look at the long list, just think of how much energy it takes to carry it around in your mind, trying to remember it all.

Is everything on the list important? If so, is it important to you, or to someone you're responsible to or for?

Must all of the items be done by you personally?

Is there a way you can automate any of these tasks, or get help with some of the tedious aspects not directly related to client contact?

If you're not good at client contact or something else required to complete a task, or if you get a sinking feeling whenever you look at something on the list, is there someone you trust who can help you, or can you get some training to improve your skills?

This is a good time to consider what Marshall Goldsmith tells his clients to ask themselves:

"What am I willing to change now? Not in a few months. Not when I get caught up. Now. Then get started on the activity within two weeks, or take it off the list. And quit tormenting yourself!" – Marshall Goldsmith

The list can and should change over time.

Clear Your Desk

You may have made your to-do list from your memory. Now look at you work area and create a clean, uncluttered, inviting place where you can work comfortably.

Social Media Mission or Purpose

Take a moment to document the working premise you're currently using for your life. You may or may not want to change anything; it's just helpful to have it in writing where you can see it more objectively.

What is your purpose in business or your personal life that leads you to investing time and money in social media?

How would you describe the successful outcome of your social media campaign? Be as specific as you can. It's okay if this changes; it's just helpful to have a clear idea of where you're starting.

What are the reasons you've chosen the goals above? Write down some words or phrases next to each that describe those reasons.

Do you notice any patterns? Write down sentences that describe patterns that also resonate with you as reflecting your mission or purpose.

Focus Session

Part of my routine every day includes what I call a Focus Session. I keep hearing how important focus is to people who have become very successful, and I find this so useful myself that I offer it to you as another tool to keep yourself on track. It's a great way to start the day before everyone else's priorities eclipse your own.

Here's my recipe:

I sit down in a quiet place with my planner and look at my values and goals, and allow myself to feel what I will experience when I actually achieve those goals.

- Then I look at what I have planned for the upcoming day, and see how closely they are aligned with my values and overall goals.

- Is everything I'm planning to do actually addressing my needs, or have I taken on responsibilities that are not mine?

- What can I add to my day to inspire me and keep me happy?

All of this takes about five minutes. I do this again throughout the day as I have time.

Attitude

How do you begin and end your day? Consider beginning the day waking up in happy anticipation of the inventive ways Life will bring new and wonderful things to you today, and ending your day reviewing what happened with gratitude and appreciation, forgiving yourself and others for any blunders and absurdities. Sometimes feelings are a choice. We can choose gratitude and curiosity rather than a host of more negative feelings. How does attitude fit into a time management chapter? We make better decisions and see more opportunities and resources when we're thinking about what could work, rather than what's wrong and who's to blame.

Systems

Do you use a planner or PDA, or are you operating from floating pieces of paper that seem to get lost regularly? Are you keeping track of your promises or are meetings and commitments falling through the cracks? When you start your day, do you know what you expect from yourself?

Use Your Planner

An easy, free way to keep track of your calendar: download Palm Desktop, which you can use even if you don't have a PDA. Alternatively use Outlook or software that comes with your PDA if you track things digitally. Keeping track on paper in an old-fashioned dependable planner also works!

How to Protect Yourself from Overwhelm

Whenever you get that feeling that it's just too much, stop whatever you're doing and allow a deep breath. Whew! The world sure is full of wonderful options and possibilities, isn't it?! My friend Marshall Goldsmith talks about 'drowning in a sea of opportunity'. It happens to all of us.

Sometimes this feeling of overwhelm is an indication we're moving into a territory we don't immediately see as aligned with our goals, and it's our inner voice trying to get our attention that we've gone off track. Or maybe we've been working for six hours straight and our blood sugar is getting low and we need some good protein and nutrition … or just a glass of water! Our brains work much better when we're hydrated. Or maybe we're scared because we don't have some bit of information or the skills to take our project to the next step.

Instead of walking away in frustration, take a quiet moment to go a little deeper into your thoughts or feelings to see what might be behind that feeling of overwhelm. If you're hungry but still on a deadline, write down two unanswered questions you're working on and carry them with you to dinner. Don't beat yourself up trying to push the answers out of yourself. Really make your dinner hour peaceful and enjoyable, and just have the paper with unanswered questions handy so you can look at it when you've rested and your mind starts naturally becoming interested again. Remember … you're on a one-hour vacation! You can work if you want, but only if you want. Just for this one hour. Or ten minutes. Whatever you can afford time-wise.

If you're getting off track, figure out where you left the main road and go back there to start. If you've gone off on a wonderful tangent and developed ideas and information you might use later, document what you've learned so far and put it in a folder for later reference. Then focus again on the main track to complete your immediate task.

If you realize you don't have enough information or the right skills to complete the next step, think about how you might get the information, how you might acquire the skills, or who might be able to help you.

If you're simply exhausted and want off the treadmill, finish whatever you need to accomplish immediately (if anything) and then schedule some time off where you really have no responsibilities except to yourself. We all have to work to make ends meet, and sometimes do things when we'd prefer to play or do work that's more interesting, but there's a limit to how much we can push ourselves. Our bodies or relationships will suffer at some point if we don't take care of our basic needs.

Think about your basic needs. As you read the next chapter Universal Needs Chart, identify your own basic needs at this point and make plans to meet them within your current frame of reference.

CHAPTER 8

Universal Needs Chart

ℰↄ

Why do I have this weird section about needs in a social media book? Quite simply because I've found this concept can save a tremendous amount of time when dealing with people, most especially with myself.

How it Works

Everyone has feelings and needs which propel them into behaviors, conclusions, choices and messages that may or may not be the best strategies to meet their needs. Most people are not conscious of which of their needs are driving them, or why they're so unhappy or unfulfilled.

Most people who react to the behaviors, conclusions, choices and messages of the people around them are also not aware of the person's needs, or their own needs as they react within their own habitual patterns.

We can spend countless hours, years and decades going around in circles explaining why it's someone else's fault, telling our same sad stories, railing against the same seemingly insurmountable conditions. The people around us can spend those same countless hours and decades debating the pros and cons with us, telling us why we shouldn't be so upset, arguing why they're not to blame and making their explanations.

Why doesn't this work? Because nobody has figured out what they really need. They're all arguing about strategies, having conflicts with what they perceive as 'the enemy'. The odd and amazing truth at the bottom of it all ... we all have the same needs. Often people locked into the most difficult conflicts share exactly the same basic, universal needs. If they can get past their stories and enemy images and actually open their hearts to hear the human being they've locked horns with, chances are each party will discover they're both fighting for safety or recognition or significance or some other universal need. When they can both recognize this and drop the rest, it's also amazing how quickly they can agree on a strategy that will work for both of them.

What does this have to do with social media and time management?

I think it's useful to shortcut the chatter and drama and be able to identify, or at least make a heartfelt guess, as to the need someone we're dealing with might be trying to meet. Then hopefully instead of becoming embroiled in the hopeless mental landscape they've invited us into, we can come from a different place and have a more productive conversation for both of us.

It's also useful to be aware of our own needs so we can make our own choices based on meeting those needs. We'll be happier and healthier, and we'll spend much less time dithering and squander fewer resources on things that on the surface seem like they'll give us the safety, recognition or signifance we're looking for, but actually just end up helping us feel a bit lonelier and more empty.

I include this list of needs because it's a useful reference when identifying the reason behind someone's behavior we don't understand, or our own feelings. When we can identify the need, we're very close to mediating conflicts, finding a solution that will work, or moving closer to a very fulfilling life.

How to Use the Chart

The following list of needs is neither exhaustive nor definitive. It is meant as a starting place to support anyone who wishes to engage in a process of deepening self-discovery and to facilitate greater understanding and connection between people.

For more information read *Conscious Networking* by Marilyn McLeod. For now, just use this list as a guide when trying to identify someone's underlying need to help you relate to them in a significant way.

Connection

acceptance
affection
appreciation
belonging
cooperation
communication
closeness
community
companionship
compassion
consideration
consistency
empathy
inclusion
intimacy
love
mutuality
nurturing
respect/self-respect
safety
security
stability

support
to know and be known
to see and be seen
to understand and
be understood
trust
warmth

Physical Wellbeing
air
food
movement/exercise
rest/sleep
sexual expression
safety
shelter
touch
water

Honesty
authenticity
integrity
presence

Play
joy
humor

Peace
beauty
communion
ease
equality
harmony
inspiration
order

Meaning

awareness
celebration of life
challenge
clarity
competence
consciousness
contribution
creativity
discovery
efficacy
effectiveness
growth
hope
learning
mourning
participation
purpose
self-expression
stimulation
to matter
understanding

Autonomy

choice
freedom
independence
space
spontaneity

Needs Chart (c) 2005 by Center for Nonviolent Communication
Website: www.cnvc.org Email: cnvc@cnvc.org
Phone: +1.505-244-4041

CHAPTER 9

Follow-Up

ℰつ

Each coach has their own area of expertise, their own personal style, and a different set of clients, so one size social media campaign doesn't fit all.

I hope I've given you the tools you need in an easy to digest form, and that you find it easy to apply what you've learned in this book.

Take one small step at a time. You've got the book as a reference, so you don't have to remember it all, or do it all.

I'd love to have you visit my website and Facebook Fan Page for this book! It's a great way for you to network … add a comment to my Fan Page discussion section and when other people visit this page they'll find you as well as me! Impart your knowledge, ask your questions, get involved in the conversation!

My online hub: http://www.CoachMarilyn.com

My email: Marilyn@CoachMarilyn.com

Check http://**www.CoachMarilyn.com** for updated resources as social media and the Internet evolve and I learn more. Add what you've learned!

Join the conversation with me and watch for updates:

http://www.Twitter.com/marilynmcleod
http://www.Facebook.com/7Steps
http://www.LinkedIn.com/in/coachmarilyn

My very best wishes to you!!!

Marilyn McLeod
Marilyn@CoachMarilyn.com
@marilynmcleod

www.ingramcontent.com/pod-product-compliance
Lightning Source LLC
Chambersburg PA
CBHW071228050326
40689CB00011B/2496